8.95

A Plains Indian Village

Other titles in the Daily Life series include:

The American Colonies

Ancient Rome

The Gold Rush

The Oregon Trail

Pirates

Daily Life

A Plains Indian Village

Stuart A. Kallen and P. M. Boekhoff

KidHaven Press

KidHaven Press, an imprint of Gale Group, Inc.

P.O. Box 289009, San Diego, CA 92198-9009

Library of Congress Cataloging-in-Publication Data

Kallen, Stuart A., 1955–
    Plains Indian village / by Stuart A. Kallen and P. M. Boekhoff.
        p. cm. — (Daily life)
    Includes bibliographical references and index.
    Summary: Discusses the Native Americans of the Great Plains in a
    historical context. Includes descriptions of their nomadic lifestyle, the
    role of women, building tipis, hunting, games, and spiritual rituals.
    ISBN 0-7377-0711-9 (alk. paper)
    1. Indians of North America—Great Plains—Material culture—
    Juvenile literature. 2. Indians of North America—Great Plains—Social
    life and customs—Juvenile literature. [1. Indians of North America—
    Great Plains—Social life and customs.] I. Boekhoff, P. M. (Patti
    Marlene), 1957– II. Title. III. Series.
    E78.G73 K35 2002
    978.004'97—dc21

    00-012857

Contents

Chapter 1

Village of Tipis

The Great Plains stretch across a large section of the central United States. From Canada in the north, the Great Plains extend deep into Texas, bordered on the east by the Mississippi River and on the west by the Rocky Mountains.

Today the Great Plains are dotted with farms and cities. But little more than a hundred years ago, the Great Plains were a vast sea of natural prairie grasses that grew up to ten feet high. The flat treeless land was marked by cold, windy winters and hot, dry summers.

In the mid-1800s, the region was populated by about 400,000 Native Americans belonging to more than thirty-two tribes. The tribes spoke a number of different languages.

The Nomadic Lifestyle

Between 1775 and 1870, the nomadic tribes of the Great Plains relied on the horse, the buffalo, and the tipi. The **nomads,** such as the Cheyenne, Crow, and Blackfoot, were hunters who lived mostly on the higher elevations of the western Great Plains, including Colorado, South

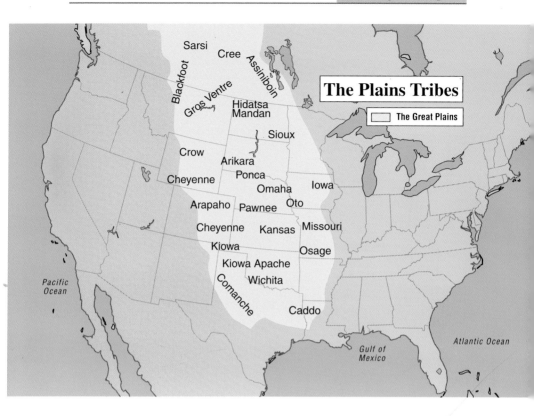

The Plains Tribes

Sarsi · Cree · Assiniboin · Blackfoot · Gros Ventre · Hidatsa · Mandan · Sioux · Crow · Arikara · Cheyenne · Ponca · Omaha · Iowa · Arapaho · Pawnee · Oto · Cheyenne · Kansas · Missouri · Kiowa · Osage · Kiowa Apache · Wichita · Comanche · Caddo

The Great Plains

Pacific Ocean · Atlantic Ocean · Gulf of Mexico

Dakota, Wyoming, and Montana. The nomadic tribes lived in small family groups, called bands.

The bands survived by hunting some of the millions of buffalo that lived on the plains. They pursued the animals on foot for centuries but quickly adapted to hunting on horseback when horses were brought to the area by Spanish explorers in the mid-1500s. Between 1775 and 1870, a pattern of life based on the horse and the buffalo emerged among nomadic tribes. By the time tens of thousands of white settlers began to move to the Great Plains in the late 1800s, the Plains tribes had a culture rich in religion, self-government, and history.

For centuries Plains tribes hunted buffalo on foot.

Living in Tipis

The nomadic tribes of the plains lived in portable tents called tipis. *Tipi*—also spelled *tepee* or *teepee*—is a Sioux word that means "used to dwell in." These structures were simple, practical, and beautiful.

The tipis and all their contents belonged to the women of the tribe. Women constructed the shelters, kept them in repair, and erected them at campsites.

The cone shape of the tipi made it safe and stable during even the harshest wind storms. The outer cover of the tipi, made from twelve to fourteen cured buffalo skins, insured that the dwelling was waterproof even in the strongest downpour. And the tipi's light weight— less than two hundred pounds—made it easy to set up, take down, and transport on horseback.

Setting Up the Tipi

A tipi's frame was made of twenty-foot-long wooden poles. The Blackfoot, Crow, and Comanche used three poles arranged in the shape of a tripod. The Dakota, Cheyenne, and Kiowa used four poles in a pyramid shape.

The three- or four-pole frame was tied together at the top with a long strip of **rawhide.** About twelve thinner poles were leaned into the top of the structure, forming a cone shape.

After the frame was constructed, women draped the buffalo skin cover over the poles. This outer shell could weigh up to 150 pounds, requiring the work of at least two women to pull it over the frame. Once in place, the cover was stretched tight around the frame and the bottom was secured to wooden stakes hammered into the ground with an elk-horn hammer.

The women then dug a fire pit in the center of the tipi and lined it with rocks. The fire provided warmth, a place to cook, and comforting light at night. The smoke from the fire rose through a circular opening at the top of the structure.

The ground under the tipi was kept dry by a liner that extended six feet up the walls. This lining was often decorated with paintings that told stories about the deeds of the women and warriors who lived within.

People entered or left the tipi through a simple doorway consisting of a hole with flaps or a triangular slit held together with narrow leather straps.

Three- or four-pole frames support the heavy outer buffalo skin shells of the tipi.

A man warms himself at the rock-lined fire pit in the center of his tipi.

How Women Made the Tipis

The hides used in making tipis were dried in the sun, which turned them a pure white color. To stitch them together, women sewed with delicate buffalo bone needles. For thread they used tightly rolled buffalo muscle, called sinew. This task was performed by the woman who owned the dwelling along with a group of friends and relatives. The entire process took one or two days.

When the cover was finished, it was put on the wood pole frame with the smoke vent closed, and a fire was built inside. This smoking process softened the hide and **cured** it, making it waterproof and turning it a cream color.

When the work was done, a feast was held to honor the women who made the tipi. Prayers were offered to ensure happiness, success, safety, and long life to the tipi owners.

Inside the Tipi

Like any typical home, tipis were the center of great activity. As many as eleven family members lived inside each structure, leaving little privacy or room for movement. Each tipi was about twenty-five feet across and fifteen feet high in the center. To hold a large family, tipis were arranged to make the best possible use of space.

Beds were aligned around the back and sides of the tipi. Backrests made from peeled willow twigs woven into a frame provided comfortable places to sit. Pillows were made from buffalo leather stuffed with fur. Furry buffalo hides were used as bedding, blankets, and rugs. Personal items were stored in rawhide bags behind the beds and next to the door.

A Plains Indian Village

An average Indian village on the plains might consist of hundreds of such tipis. The villages were set up according to religious customs that placed great value on the

Working with buffalo skin and wooden poles, women of the plains provided shelter for their families.

rising sun in the east. As such, the doorways of each individual tipi faced east, and villages were arranged in semicircles that opened on the east side.

Within the circle, tipis were set up according to family and tribal relationships. The tipis of chiefs, bravest warriors, dancers, and other high-ranking people were placed within the interior of the circle. The very center of the village was occupied by a **council lodge** used for tribal meetings. This arrangement was used each time the tribe set up camp. For this reason, hunters who were away from the camps for many months knew exactly where to find their homes when they returned.

The tipi of the Plains peoples was one of the most clever shelters ever invented. It was lightweight and could be set up in a few minutes. The **translucent** skin allowed light in during the day yet kept out wind, rain, ice, and snow. Working with only buffalo skin and wooden poles, the women of the plains provided shelter for their families in an often harsh climate.

Chapter 2

Survival on the Plains

While women provided shelter with buffalo hides, men hunted and killed buffalo with bows and arrows. This task required skill and bravery. Buffalo are massive animals more than six feet tall and weighing up to two thousand pounds. Their tough hides are not easily pierced by an arrow, and their sharp, curved horns can easily kill a man. Buffalo roamed in herds that might number in the millions. And one frightened animal could start a terrifying **stampede** that would trample anyone or anything in the way. To reduce the danger, buffalo hunts were very organized rituals in which certain rules were followed to insure the safety of the hunters.

Hunting Buffalo

The Plains hunters used their knowledge of buffalo behavior to help them with their task. During the warm seasons of the year, buffalo did not pack tightly together in large herds. Instead, they spread out over the grasslands and ate all morning. By noon many sat down and went to sleep in the midday sun. This was the best time to attack, and at a given signal the hunters moved their horses into action. Each man picked out one or two buffalo to chase with their highly trained ponies, galloping as close to the animals as possible.

As the startled buffalo began to scatter in all directions, skilled hunters shot very quickly at close range, killing one buffalo after another until all their arrows were used up. A skilled hunter could shoot five arrows in thirty seconds, and each hunter had special markings on his arrows, so he could identify which buffalo he had killed.

Plains hunters knew that the best time to attack was when the buffalo were resting.

At a given signal, hunters riding highly trained horses chase the buffalo.

Soon the women, children, and **elders** arrived to butcher the dead buffalo. The meat was cut from the animals, sliced into pieces, and wrapped in buffalo skins to be carried back to camp.

After a hunt, one dead buffalo was left behind as a religious offering. Its skin was removed and kept as a sacred object, while the remainder of the animal was left where it had fallen. The Indians believed that the animal's spirit would allow the tribes successful hunts in the future.

Buffalo Meat and Other Foods

After a successful buffalo hunt, a feast was held. Prayers of thanksgiving were offered before people gorged themselves on ribs, steak, tongue, hump, and other tasty morsels roasted over the open fire. The sweet nutritious bone marrow was saved for the elders, since it was easy to chew. One buffalo supplied enough food to feed a hundred hungry people.

After the feast, the rest of the meat was divided equally among all members of the tribe. This meat was cut into strips by the women and hung on wooden racks in the sun for several days. This sun-dried meat, called jerky, would not spoil for months. It was a light and nutritious food and could be carried anywhere.

As they traveled across the prairie on the trail of the buffalo, the nomadic tribes also added wild fruits and vegetables to their diets. Women gathered chokecherries, plums, prairie turnips, rose hips, and the fruit of the yucca plant. Dried corn, squash, beans, and tobacco were obtained by trading with tribes from the more fertile regions to the east.

Buffalo Skins

In addition to food, the buffalo provided nearly every other item needed for survival. After a buffalo was butchered, women began the long, difficult work of tanning buffalo hides. First the hides were stretched out on the ground and tied tightly to stakes. If they were to be used for rugs, blankets, or beds, the fur was left on and the flesh was scraped off the underside with

Women made jerky by cutting the meat into strips and hanging it in the sun for several days.

a bone or stone tool. If they were to be used to make tipis or moccasins, they were scraped carefully on both sides to remove all hair and flesh.

The skinned hides were soaked in a mixture of buffalo brains, fat, and liver to soften them. The hides were scraped and soaked once again, then left for two days to bleach in the sun. Finally, the hides were ready to be made into dozens of items.

In addition to supplying their families with hides, women of the tribe donated extras to the sick, old, or orphaned. In this way, every person in the tribe had enough buffalo leather to take care of their needs.

Plains Clothing

The buffalo robe was the most important clothing item to tribes living in the central and northern plains. This robe was a combination of a winter coat and a warm blanket. It was worn with the fur on the inside and the softened leather on the outside. With natural dyes made from berries and minerals, women decorated their robes with **geometric** designs. Men painted important events such as hunts and wars on their robes.

The finest robes were made from buffalo killed in winter, when the fur was long and thick. These hides were also used to make caps, leggings, earmuffs, mittens, and other items needed for the cold, bitter winters on the Great Plains. The thick, rough skin found on the necks of old bull buffalo provided tough material used for the soles of winter moccasins.

For summer clothing, people of the plains preferred lighter clothing made from deer, elk, or antelope skins. This soft supple leather was used to make men's clothing such as fringed shirts, leggings, and loincloths.

Women wore skirts and shirts, simple dresses, and knee-length leggings. Clothing of both genders was

A man's buffalo robe is decorated with a painting of an important battle.

often decorated with fringe, beads, shells, bells, porcupine quills, and even the teeth and tails of animals. Clothing styles reflected individual tastes, creativity, and the wealth of the wearer.

The Useful Buffalo

The tools for making clothing—and almost all other items—came from the different parts of the buffalo. Bones were carved into knives, spears, sewing needles, sewing awls (pointed instruments for punching holes in hides so they could be sewn together), and hide scrapers.

Horns, found on both male and female buffalo, were used to make spoons, ladles, and cups. Hooves were cooked to make glue. The fat of the buffalo was used to make soap. Dried buffalo bladders were used to hold water. Sinew was used to make bowstrings as well as sewing thread. Buffalo hair was braided into rope and bridles and was used as stuffing for dolls, balls, pillows, and other items. On the northern plains, the

Buffalo bones were carved into various tools such as the hoe seen here.

backbones and ribs were used to make snow sleds for the children.

Even buffalo droppings were useful. Firewood was scarce on the treeless plains, but a huge supply of sun-dried buffalo dung provided slow-burning, hot fires perfect for cooking, as well as warming and lighting the tipi.

Exciting Lives

The days of the Plains people were filled with the work of hunting, butchering, cooking, and sewing. While this work was demanding, tribal life was also exciting. People lived their lives on the move. Their clothing styles were only limited by their imaginations. The thrill of the hunt filled their days, while nights were spent playing games and listening to stories by the light of the campfire or watching stars. While few people today could imagine such an existence, it was the way of life for centuries under the big sky of the Great Plains.

Chapter 3

Fun and Games

When the people of the plains finished their work, they often played games. Boys played hunting and warrior games, and girls played house with dolls. Adults and children competed in running, wrestling, archery, and other games. And most grown-ups gambled on dice games, horse races, and other contests.

Games Children Play

Even from early childhood, the play of Native American boys and girls also had a purpose. Fun was found in imitating the hard work of adults. Little girls made small toy tipis and arranged them in a circle, and held feasts with make-believe food. They filled the tipis with stuffed deerskin dolls dressed in clothes that their mothers sewed. And the dolls were also put in tiny baby cradles that were similar to the real cradles their mothers carried on their backs.

Like their fathers, little boys practiced shooting toy bows and arrows. To develop skills they would need later in life, they pretended to go on buffalo hunts while

Adults gambled on horse races and other games of chance.

riding stick horses. Other boys played the buffalo, carrying prickly pear leaves on sticks. An arrow shot into a mark on the prickly pear was a buffalo kill, and the boy playing the buffalo would fall down and play dead. If the arrow missed, the enraged buffalo would charge, perhaps hitting the hunter on his rear with a prickly cactus.

Children also played simpler games with spinning tops and animal figures carved from wood. Like all children, they played tag, hide-and-seek, and ball games. Older boys staged wrestling matches and ran footraces.

By the time they were six years old, boys and girls had their own ponies to ride. At this age, however, boys and girls were separated. Boys were given their first real bows and arrows and practiced hunting on small animals such as squirrels and birds. Girls went to work to help their mothers in their daily chores.

Fighting and Hunting

Before they were teenagers, both boys and girls learned to defend themselves if attacked by enemies, but boys also spent many days playing war games. Like a football game with no ball, young boys divided into teams, charged at each other, and tried to knock one another to the ground. This game was also played with opponents trying to wrestle each other off horses. These contests produced lumps and bruises but toughened the would-be warriors. Once a youngster had learned bravery and strength at play, he began to use his skills in real life.

When they were twelve to fourteen years old, young men learned to hunt from their fathers and uncles.

Teenage boys around twelve to fourteen years of age went on their first real buffalo hunts with their fathers and uncles. The young men learned to follow buffalo footprints and broken **vegetation** to track the herd. When a boy killed his first buffalo, usually a young calf, his father joyously shouted the news to the whole village. If his family could afford it, they celebrated by giving a good horse to a deserving poor person or by giving a feast for the less fortunate in the tribe.

Girls Gather Herbs, Cook, and Sew

As girls grew into young women, they stayed near the tipi and did not go out alone. They learned how to sew and decorate clothing, gather and dry wild foods, and cook. They mastered the traditional crafts of women, such as painting on rawhide and porcupine-quill embroidery.

Girls competed in developing their artistic skills. If a girl became very skilled, she would be allowed to join a craft workers' guild for women. This gave her the right to make special religious items for the tribe.

Adult Games

Games and competitions were not played solely by young people. Every spring and fall, friendly tribes met to compete in games such as footraces, wrestling matches, archery contests, and ball games. These games were part of meetings, or powwows, that included religious ceremonies, feasting, and trading.

Horse races were some of the most popular contests among the tribes. And before their horses ran a four-mile course, warriors might bet everything they owned on their favorite ponies. Judges were always present to ensure fair play.

Another popular sport was a racket ball game, named lacrosse by French fur traders. In modern

Horse races were the most popular contests among tribes.

lacrosse, two teams, each with ten players, use long-handled sticks with webbed pouches to throw a ball into goals about 120 feet apart. In the original game, a team consisted of hundreds, even thousands, of men and women players—maybe even an entire village or tribe. The goals were set several miles apart and the game might last up to three days.

Players were not allowed to touch the ball with their hands. Instead, the rackets were used to catch, carry, or throw the ball into the other team's goal at the end of the field. Since most players never even saw the ball, they simply used their sticks to strike opponents. For this reason, lacrosse was considered good practice for war.

Lacrosse matches consisted of hundreds, even thousands, of men and women players.

The huge matches attracted thousand of spectators, who bet heavily on the outcome. Players trained for months before a big game, and dances and ceremonies were held to bring strength and success to the players.

Learning from Play

The strong spirit of competition seen in the Plains people began at a very young age. Childhood games taught important lessons for adulthood. And skills learned by adults in horse races or lacrosse matches could be useful in times of war. Just as the Plains tribes used every part of the buffalo, they did not waste energy even when playing. Instead, while waging contests against their friends, the people of the plains trained for the serious business of life.

Chapter 4

Honoring the Spirits

The Native Americans on the plains were deeply spiritual people with strong religious views. They believed that everything in their natural world was alive with spirits. These spirits were said to govern the actions of all plants, animals, rocks, and the weather.

The natural spirits were ruled by a supreme god called the Great Spirit. This god gave order to life, aided harmony between people, and kept humans in balance with nature. The Great Spirit was all-powerful and present everywhere. The Great Spirit promised a world beyond death where people would live forever. And this spirit was in every person in every group.

The people of the plains did not separate religion from everyday life. The tribes held dozens of **rituals** and festivals throughout the year that included singing, dancing, and drumming. Rituals were held to honor the spirits, ensure successful hunts, and gain victory in battle. Celebrations came when babies were born or when an enemy was conquered.

Rituals of singing, dancing, and drumming honor the spirits, ensure successful hunts, and gain victory in battle.

The Vision Quest

The power of the Great Spirit was thought to be beyond normal human understanding. People could communicate with the spirit world, however, by living in a sacred manner. The people of the plains believed that the spirits could instruct them through dreams and visions. To receive such a vision, people participated in several types of religious rituals.

This isolated lodge is the sort of place a young person may have gone to wait for a vision.

A vision quest was usually undertaken by boys and girls around twelve to fourteen years of age, and it was one of the deepest religious experiences in a person's life. At this age, parents would escort their children to an isolated hilltop. Some built small lodges or a platform in a tree where the child would be assured of total isolation. After the parents left, the youngster waited for a vision. The seeker was allowed a small amount of water, but absolutely no food for the first five days. Starvation and isolation often brought on strange dreams or hallucinations.

Children who fasted were believed to arouse the pity of the spirits and in most cases were granted a vision that would guide them through life. Typically a person on a vision quest would see a being that might take many forms—animal, human, or **supernatural.** Visions could also include a plant, object, place, ancestor, or natural event, such as a storm. The being often spoke to the seeker, offering compassion, insight, good fortune, and spiritual guidance. After the vision quest was over, children returned to their lodges for celebrations and feasts. Because visions were considered private and sacred, they were only discussed with a father, mother, or spiritual leader. These adults helped the children to understand the mysteries of the vision.

Ceremonial Dancing

Vision quest celebrations were followed by hours of dancing around a campfire. Dance was believed to preserve the life force of the entire tribe, and dancing was a very important part of all Plains Indians ceremonies. Dance music was played on drums, rattles, flutes, whistles, and similar instruments. Some dancers mimicked animal or bird calls.

Tribes expressed emotions such as sorrow, bravery, ecstasy, **valor,** love, and devotion to the Great Spirit through dance. They also portrayed past history, such as hunting adventures and successful battles. There were dances for curing the sick, performing magic, playing games, courting, and influencing nature.

Plains Indians play music on drums, rattles, whistles, and flutes (pictured).

Male dancers perform the buffalo dance before a hunt.

For example, the buffalo dance was used to influence nature. This ritual was performed to attract buffalo close to the camp circle, where they could be easily killed. Before the hunt, male dancers in buffalo masks pawed, stampeded, and milled about, imitating the movements of the buffalo. Sometimes the dance went on for days, as new dancers stepped in to replace those who had tired. During the performance of the dance, young men left the circle in search of buffalo herds.

Singing was as important as dancing during religious ceremonies and rituals. Composers often received their songs through dreams or visions. Such songs were valued for their power to allow access to the spirit realm. Religious songs were passed down from generation to generation to use in ceremonies. Songs were believed to bring healing, good weather, and success in hunting and war.

Medicine

The Plains Indians believed that the spiritual powers of song and dance came from the Great Spirit. This power was called medicine and was believed to have influence over events.

To give them protection at all times, people put together bags called medicine bundles that held what were believed to be magical items. When the people of the plains fell ill or had bad luck, they usually looked for the cure in their personal medicine bundle. Medicinal substances such as herbs and spices and sacred objects such as rattles and sacred pipes were kept in the medicine bundles. If the answer or cure was not in the medicine bundle, a doctor, or medicine man, was called.

Doctors used herbs, chants, songs, dances, and even hypnosis to effect their cures. Most tribes had a variety of doctors with different skills, such as herbalists, midwives to deliver babies, and specialists in such procedures as setting bones or treating wounds.

A shaman dresses in an elaborate costume to treat an illness of the spirit.

If the illness was spiritual rather than physical, a priest was called. Known as a shaman, this holy man purified himself for days before performing a healing. To effect a cure, he might dress in an elaborate costume while performing a healing ceremony. For instance, the shaman might wear an entire bearskin from head to toe, with the skins of smaller animals hanging from it.

Sometimes shamans were given gifts for their services. But medicine men did not often keep the riches they earned. Instead, they gave the gifts to others in order to earn respect by acting in a noble manner. To the people of the plains, wealth was measured not by what a person had, but by what they shared with others.

A modern-day medicine man attempts to heal an elderly woman.

Making War

Medicine was often used to cure the sick. It was also believed to bring luck to the tribe during war. Medicine men would peer into the future and try to pick the best time and place for battle. And injured warriors were brought to shamans to be healed.

Plains Indians were fearless men who had a warrior tradition dating back to prehistoric times. War was as much a part of life on the Great Plains as hunting buffalo. Success in battle was the way a man gained wealth and respect. And great warriors were forever remembered in the legends of their tribe.

When warriors of the plains clashed in battle, bows were drawn and arrows rained down on the enemy from a distance. After the initial clash, the men moved in for hand-to-hand combat.

When a war party returned to its village, the men let out special whoops or cries to let people know if they had been successful or not. After the battle, the village celebrated with feasts, singing, and dancing.

From Birth to Death

The people of the plains carried out rituals for every aspect of life from birth to death. The spirits, healing, and medicine of the natural world were as important to them as the air they breathed and the food they ate. From the vision quest to the buffalo dance, these spirits helped the Plains people survive in a harsh environment that was often uncertain and dangerous.

Glossary

council lodge: A place where people come together to decide important matters.

cure: To preserve by smoking or salting.

elder: A respected older member of a tribe, family, or community.

geometric: Using the forms of geometry, such as circles, squares, and triangles.

nomads: People who move their homes according to the seasons in search of food and water.

rawhide: An animal hide that has not been cured or dried in the sun.

ritual: The acts performed in a religious ceremony.

stampede: A sudden rush of animals.

supernatural: A divine power outside of the natural world.

translucent: Almost transparent, allowing some light through so that objects can be seen but not very clearly.

valor: Courage, boldness, bravery, as in battle.

vegetation: The plant life of an area or region.

For Further Exploration

Elaine Andrews, *Indians of the Plains.* New York: Facts On File, 1992. A book about the rich and varied culture and history of the Plains tribes.

Gordon C. Baldwin, *Games of the American Indian.* New York: W. W. Norton, 1969. A detailed book on the many kinds of games played by Native American children.

Russell Freedman, *Buffalo Hunt.* New York: Holiday House, 1988. A beautiful book about the Native American buffalo hunt on the Great Plains vividly illustrated with paintings by George Catlin and other artists who traveled the West in the nineteenth century.

Robert Hofsinde (Grey-Wolf), *The Indian Medicine Man.* New York: William Morrow, 1966. A detailed book about Sioux, Iroquois, Apache, Ojibwa, and other medicine men written by a Native American author.

Earle Rice Jr., *Life Among the Great Plains Indians.* San Diego: Lucent Books, 1998. This book shows an honest and complete picture of the Plains culture in the 1800s.

Lisa Sita, *Indians of the Great Plains: Traditions, History, Legends, and Life.* Philadelphia: Running Press, 1997. A book that explores the lives and legends of the peoples who inhabited the Great Plains, including their social activities, spiritual customs, and governmental systems.

Michael Bad Hand Terry, *Daily Life in a Plains Indian Village 1868.* New York: Houghton Mifflin, 1999. A fascinating and detailed look at the daily life of a Plains Indian family more than 130 years ago. Chapters cover the duties of each family member, including the children, and their roles in the community.

David and Charlotte Yue, *The Tipi.* New York: Alfred A. Knopf, 1984. An entire book about tipis and the people who built them and lived in them.

Index

Picture Credits

About the Authors

Stuart A. Kallen is the author of more than 150 nonfiction books for children and young adults. He has written extensively about Native Americans and American history. In addition, Mr. Kallen has written award-winning children's videos and television scripts. In his spare time, Stuart A. Kallen is a singer/songwriter/guitarist in San Diego, California.

P. M. Boekhoff is a professional artist who has cocreated several children's books on the subjects of art and ecology and illustrated many book covers. In her spare time, she writes poetry and studies herbal medicine.